When I Am Gloomy
울적한 날에

Sam Sagolski
Illustrated by Daria Smyslova

www.kidkiddos.com
Copyright ©2025 by KidKiddos Books Ltd.
support@kidkiddos.com

All rights reserved. No part of this book may be reproduced in any form or by any electronic or mechanical means, including information storage and retrieval systems, without written permission from the publisher, except in the case of a reviewer, who may quote brief passages embodied in critical articles or in a review.
First edition, 2025

Translated from English by Jinyeong Jung
정진영 옮김

Library and Archives Canada Cataloguing in Publication
When I Am Gloomy (English Korean Bilingual edition)/Shelley Admont
ISBN: 978-1-83416-801-2 paperback
ISBN: 978-1-83416-802-9 hardcover
ISBN: 978-1-83416-800-5 eBook

Please note that the English and Korean versions of the story have been written to be as close as possible. However, in some cases they differ in order to accommodate nuances and fluidity of each language.

One cloudy morning, I woke up feeling gloomy.

어느 흐린 날 아침, 울적한 기분으로 잠에서 깼어요.

I got out of bed, wrapped myself in my favorite blanket, and walked into the living room.

나는 침대에서 나와, 제일 좋아하는 이불로 몸을 감싸고는, 거실로 걸어 나왔어요.

"Mommy!" I called. "I'm in a bad mood."

"엄마!" 내가 말했어요. "기분이 안 좋아요."

Mom looked up from her book. "Bad? Why do you say that, darling?" she asked.

엄마는 책에서 눈을 떼고 고개를 들었어요. "기분이 안 좋다니? 왜 그러니, 우리 아가?" 엄마가 물었어요.

"Look at my face!" I said, pointing to my furrowed brows. Mom smiled gently.

"내 표정 좀 보세요!" 나는 찡그린 눈썹을 가리키며 말했어요. 엄마는 다정하게 미소 지었어요.

"I don't have a happy face today," I mumbled. "Do you still love me when I'm gloomy?"

"오늘은 행복한 표정이 아닌 걸요." 나는 웅얼거리며 물었어요. "내가 울적한 날에도 엄마는 나를 사랑해요?"

"Of course I do," Mom said. "When you're gloomy, I want to be close to you, give you a big hug, and cheer you up."

"그럼, 당연하지." 엄마가 말했어요. "울적한 날에는 엄마가 옆에서 꼭 안아주면서 기운이 나도록 해 주고 싶단다."

That made me feel a little better, but only for a second, because then I started thinking about all my other moods.

그 말에 기분이 조금 나아졌지만, 잠시 뿐이었어요. 왜냐하면 나의 다른 기분들이 생각났거든요.

"So… do you still love me when I'm angry?"
"그럼… 내가 화났을 때도 나를 사랑해요?"

Mom smiled again. "Of course I do!"
엄마는 또다시 빙긋 웃었어요. "그렇고 말고!"

"Are you sure?" I asked, crossing my arms.
"정말로요?" 나는 팔짱을 끼며 물었어요.

"Even when you're mad, I'm still your mom. And I love you just the same."

"네가 화가 나더라도 나는 언제나 네 엄마야. 그럴 때도 변함없이 널 사랑해."

I took a big breath. "What about when I'm shy?" I whispered.

나는 숨을 깊이 들이마셨어요. "그럼 내가 부끄러워할 때는요?" 나는 속삭였어요.

"I love you when you're shy too," she said. "Remember when you hid behind me and didn't want to talk to the new neighbor?"

"네가 부끄러워할 때에도 엄마는 널 사랑해." 엄마가 말했어요. "네가 엄마 뒤에 숨어서 새 이웃한테 말을 안 걸고 싶어했던 때 기억나니?"

I nodded. I remembered it well.

나는 고개를 끄덕였어요. 그때를 똑똑히 기억하고 있었거든요.

"And then you said hello and made a new friend. I was so proud of you."

"그래도 네가 인사를 건네고 새 친구를 사귀었잖니. 네가 정말 자랑스러웠단다."

"Do you still love me when I ask too many questions?" I continued.

"내가 궁금한 게 엄청 많아도 엄마는 날 사랑해요?" 나는 계속해서 물었어요.

"When you ask a lot of questions, like now, I get to watch you learn new things that make you smarter and stronger every day," Mom answered. "And yes, I still love you."

"지금처럼 네가 궁금한 게 많을 땐 말이야, 엄마는 하루하루 네가 새로운 걸 배우면서 똑똑하고 강해지는 모습을 지켜볼 수 있어." 엄마가 대답했어요. "그러니까 엄마는 여전히 너를 사랑해."

"What if I don't feel like talking at all?" I continued asking.

"그럼 내가 아무 말도 안 하고 싶으면요?" 나는 계속 질문했어요.

"Come here," she said. I climbed into her lap and rested my head on her shoulder.

"이리 오렴." 엄마가 말했어요. 나는 엄마 무릎 위로 올라가 엄마 어깨에 머리를 기댔어요.

"When you don't feel like talking and just want to be quiet, you start using your imagination. I love seeing what you create," Mom answered.

"아무 말 없이 그냥 조용히 있고 싶은 날, 너는 상상의 나래를 펼치고 있을 거야. 엄마는 네가 무엇을 만들어내는지 바라보는 일이 참 좋아." 엄마가 대답했어요.

Then she whispered in my ear, "I love you when you're quiet too."

그런 다음 엄마가 내 귀에 속삭였어요. "네가 조용할 때에도 엄마는 널 사랑해."

"But do you still love me when I'm afraid?" I asked.
"그렇지만 내가 무서워할 때도 날 사랑해요?" 내가 물었어요.

"Always," said Mom. "When you're scared, I help you check that there are no monsters under the bed or in the closet."
"언제든지 사랑하지." 엄마가 말했어요. "무서울 땐 엄마가 침대 밑이나 옷장 속에 괴물이 없는지 살펴봐 줄게."

She kissed me on the forehead. "You are so brave, my sweetheart."

엄마가 내 이마에 뽀뽀를 하며 말했어요. "우리 아가, 넌 정말 용감하단다."

"And when you're tired," she added softly, "I cover you with your blanket, bring you your teddy bear, and sing you our special song."

"그리고 네가 지쳤을 땐 말이야." 엄마가 부드럽게 이야기했어요. "엄마가 이불을 덮어주고, 곰인형을 갖다 준 다음, 우리만의 특별한 노래를 불러 줄게."

"What if I have too much energy?" I asked, jumping to my feet.

"내 힘이 넘치는 날에는요?" 나는 벌떡 일어나며 물었어요.

She laughed. "When you're full of energy, we go biking, skip rope, or run around outside together. I love doing all those things with you!"

엄마는 웃었어요. "힘이 넘치는 날에는 자전거를 타거나, 줄넘기를 하거나, 밖에서 같이 뛰어놀자. 엄마는 이 모든 걸 너와 함께 하는 게 정말 좋아!"

"But do you love me when I don't want to eat broccoli?" I stuck out my tongue.

"그럼 내가 브로콜리 먹는 걸 싫어해도 엄마는 날 사랑해요?" 나는 혀를 삐죽 내밀었어요.

Mom chuckled. "Like that time you slipped your broccoli to Max? He liked it a lot."

엄마는 싱긋 웃었어요. "네가 맥스한테 브로콜리를 슬쩍 넘겨줬을 때처럼? 맥스가 브로콜리를 되게 좋아하더라."

"You saw that?" I asked.
"엄마도 봤어요?" 내가 물었어요.

"Of course I did. And I still love you, even then."
"그럼, 당연하지. 그리고 그럴 때도 엄마는 널 사랑해."

I thought for a moment, then asked one last question:
나는 잠시 생각하고는 마지막으로 한 가지를 물어봤어요.

"Mommy, if you love me when I'm gloomy or mad… do you still love me when I'm happy?"
"엄마, 엄마는 내가 울적하거나 화가 나더라도 날 사랑한다고 했잖아요… 그럼 내가 행복할 때도 날 사랑해요?"

"Oh, sweetheart," she said, hugging me again, "when you're happy, I'm happy too."
"오, 우리 아가." 엄마가 다시 나를 안아주며 말했어요. "네가 행복하면 엄마도 행복해."

She kissed me on the forehead and added, "I love you when you're happy just as much as I love you when you're sad, or mad, or shy, or tired."
엄마는 내 이마에 뽀뽀를 하고는 이렇게 말했어요. "엄마는 네가 슬플 때, 화가 났을 때, 부끄러울 때, 지쳤을 때만큼 네가 행복할 때에도 너를 사랑한단다."

I snuggled close and smiled. "So... you love me all the time?" I asked.

나는 엄마 품으로 파고들면서 활짝 웃었어요. "그럼… 엄마는 언제든지 나를 사랑하는 거예요?" 내가 물었어요.

"All the time," she said. "Every mood, every day, I love you always."

"언제든지." 엄마가 말했어요. "네가 어떤 기분이든, 매일매일 엄마는 널 항상 사랑해."

As she spoke, I started feeling something warm in my heart.

엄마 말에 마음 속에서 무언가 따뜻해지는 게 느껴졌어요.

I looked outside and saw the clouds floating away. The sky was turning blue, and the sun came out.

바깥을 보니 구름이 걷히고 있었어요. 하늘은 파랗게 물들었고, 해가 모습을 나타냈어요.

It looked like it was going to be a beautiful day after all.

결국에는 화창한 하루가 될 것 같아 보였어요.

www.ingramcontent.com/pod-product-compliance
Lightning Source LLC
LaVergne TN
LVHW072009060526
838200LV00010B/307